Oslo's Melbourne

Illustrated adventures in the world's most tolerated city

OSLO DAVIS

Black Inc.

'Jesus, this city! The construction! The people! The haircuts!'

—Anonymous, Collins Street

Introduction

I'M PRETTY MUCH THE WORST AUTHORITY on
Melbourne you can get. I get on the wrong trams, I panic
then muddle my order at Brunetti's, and I still don't know
the difference between a latte and a flat white (if there really
is one, let's face it).

Moreover, I don't tend to 'explore new precincts' or 'lose
myself in the city' (both of which sound like euphemisms
for passing out drunk on a bus). It would practically take a
death in the family or a crazy-cheap deal on Gumtree to make
me leave my beloved inner-west suburb. You could say I have
a complicated, love/hate/tolerate relationship with Melbourne,
where 'fear of living in any place that's not Melbourne' is
pretty much the only thing keeping me here.*

So when my publisher suggested I put together a nice little
book of my Melbourne drawings, my initial reaction was
that they must have got me confused with Shaun Tan. What
the hell do I know about Melbourne? I was born in northern
Tasmania, only arriving in Melbourne in my thirties.

But as I image-searched old hard drives, rifled through stacks
of drawings and downloaded attachments from ancient
emails to newspaper editors, I discovered I had done an
embarrassingly excessive amount of work about Melbourne.

You would think I actually liked the place.

Melbourne in the early 2000s was booming and quite sure of itself. Yet I also remember everything here feeling a touch over-hyped. Drawing pictures that ridiculed Melbourne's contradictions was probably my way to connect and engage, and to bring the city down a peg or two.

Oslo's Melbourne was assembled over a couple of lockdowns, when I could pry myself off the internet. Many are new works done for this book and others are old favourites remastered for clarity.

Looking over it now with a degree of distance, it's still a mystery why those editors and art directors asked a non-authority to draw about Melbourne. But I'm willing to trust their judgement and hang around this city for a while longer, even if it's because living somewhere else is too frightening.

Oslo Davis

---

* OK, OK, that's not completely true. Melbourne has more than a few redeeming features. Namely: the fig ice cream at Jock's in Albert Park; how you can go 70 km/h on Dynon Road; the College of Surgeons building at the top of Lonsdale Street; those soft-shelled tacos at La Tortilleria; the ABC TV News team; the yellow-tailed black cockatoos that roost along the Maribyrnong River; how cramped it is in The Paperback Bookshop. But that's about it.

Your Typical
Melbourne Day.
by Oslo Davis

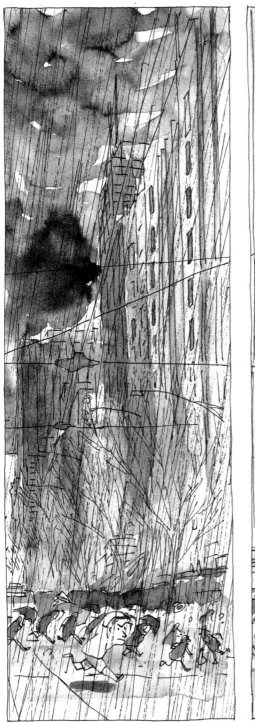

Wish You Were Here

During a couple of lockdowns, I drew more than 400 random pictures and cartoons on postcards. People ordered them online, not knowing what they would get, pot-luck style. Some drawings were pretty, some were wacky. My thinking at the time was, as it is now, absurdity and nonsense are the only things that will save us.

GREETINGS FROM

RINGWOOD!

MY LATE UNCLE WAS A SPANISH COWBOY

(NEVER LIKED HIM)

PUFFIN'

I HAVE FOND MEMORIES OF FAMILY HOLIDAYS

IN HOPPERS CROSSING

MY BROTHER WAS FEARLESS

(THIS IS NOT MY BROTHER)

HAVE NEVER TRUSTED

MEN IN FLAT CAPS

GREETINGS FROM NIDDRIE!

THE WATER SKIING CAPITAL

MAN OF THE DUNES

(DON'T GO NEAR HIM)

UNCLE RAY

JUST AS ANNOYING IN 3D

GREETINGS from

OUYEN

THERE IS VERY LITTLE CORAL

IN THE MARIBYRNONG

Melbhattan

In a time before the name 'Woody Allen' poisoned everything it touched, I spent a good part of a year creating a short animation titled *Melbhattan* — a pastiche of the grand montage of New York that opens Allen's 1979 film, *Manhattan*.

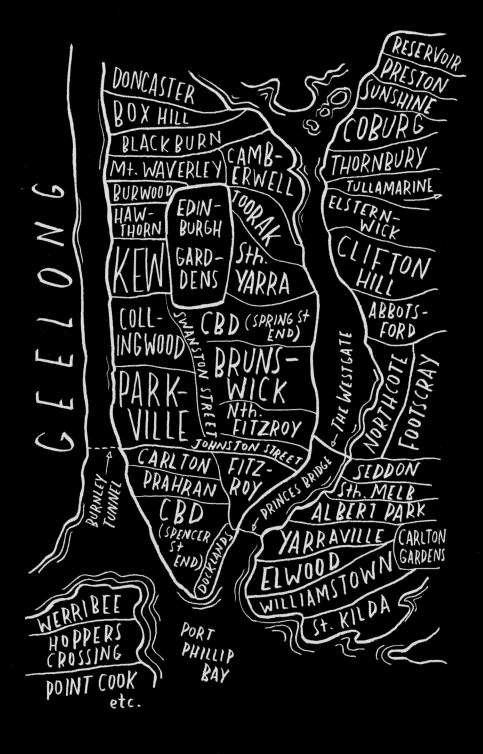

IT'S NOT REALLY MY THING TO BE SENTIMENTAL. So my goal with *Melbhattan* was not to celebrate Melbourne, but to kind of ridicule the sizeable proportion of inner-city Melburnians who think our city is a mini Manhattan. However, after I made *Melbhattan*, and saw it with thousands of others at the Palais during the opening of the 2013 St Kilda Film Festival, I realised I may have made something a bit sentimental after all.

I first saw *Manhattan* in 1987, when I was fifteen, and cinematographer Gordon Willis's rich, epic black-and-white opening montage had a big impact on me. From the initial clarinet glissando of George Gershwin's 'Rhapsody in Blue', the viewer is hurried through sixty-one shots of New York: street-smart guys and beautiful women; construction sites; harbour ferries; market vendors; Upper East Side school kids tumbling out of class; the Lincoln Center, Yankee Stadium, Radio City and Times Square at night; a collection of out-of-this-world long shots over Central Park as the sun sets behind the skyscrapers; and ending with Fourth of July fireworks over the famous skyline.

The idea that Melbourne is an antipodean Manhattan is not a new one, but after my wife and I returned from a stint in Tokyo, it seemed Melbourne was trying to be more like New York than ever. It was 2003 and the people here seemed richer, pushier and crankier.

Everyone was banging on about how the cultural capital of Australia was now the most liveable city in the world. The Brooklyn hipster movement was taking hold in Collingwood. People were only half-joking when they called the areas north and south of Johnston Street NoJo and SoJo, and developers began building an Upper West Side tower on King Street and flogging 'New York–style studio apartments' on Flinders Lane.

Former Melbourne Writers Festival director Steve Grimwade, who made *The New Yorker* magazine a focus of one of his festivals, said that 'Melburnians have looked ... to places they can aspire to be like and, in many ways, New York is that city.'

I liked this conscious-or-not aspiration to be a type of New York, but as a cartoonist I had an obligation to keep that adoration in check. It was this thinking that inspired me to cast Melbourne as New York in the style of Allen's *Manhattan*, to both charm and roast my new home without being too mean.

I began making *Melbhattan* by printing out every shot of *Manhattan*'s opening montage, and then scouted Melbourne for comparable locations. I photographed the MCG from the Sofitel toilets at night to evoke Yankee Stadium. I snapped the central business district from the top of the Shrine of Remembrance, over the trees of the Royal Botanic Gardens,

to mimic Willis's long shots over Central Park. Prada on Collins Street was Bloomingdales, the Manchester Unity Building was any neo-Gothic building on Broadway.

I then drew each scene using a fine-tipped pen before applying ink wash and assembling the sixty-one frames on a computer. The moving bits – a car passing, someone walking their dog through Fitzroy Gardens – were animated in jumpy steps of three or four.

Gershwin, speaking of how he conceived 'Rhapsody in Blue' in 1924, said he 'heard it as a sort of musical kaleidoscope of America, of our vast melting pot, of our unduplicated national pep … our metropolitan madness'. Biddy Connor, a local composer, took on the task of making the music for *Melbhattan* – a new soundtrack for Melbourne, just as 'Rhapsody' had become for New York. Like me, Biddy tried to keep the romanticism of the original from infecting our attempts at parody.

My *Melbhattan* became a battle to keep the work aligned to that initial, perfect one-second flash of an idea: a good-natured teasing of Melbourne. But in its place grew something else: a nervy, twitchy animation that shows that perhaps I am a little too sentimental about Melbourne, even though I try not to be about almost everything else.

Art

Drawings from Melbourne, the supposed
'creative capital' of Australia

Oslo DAVIS
Australia 1972—

Up for Grabs, an Arkley!
After Howard Arkley's *A Splendid
    Superior Home* (1989). From
    Davis's series 'Improvements
    On Australian Art'
2014 Melbourne
oil on canvas

HOW TO SPOT A MELBOURNE ART WANKER A MILE OFF

PREPOSTEROUS EYEWEAR

LEGS AKIMBO

CARRYING DESIGNER DOGS

PATHETICALLY UNIRONIC HAIRCUTS

HAUGHTY, CONCEITED RACONTEURING

SELF-DELUDEDLY PURPORTS TO ACTUALLY LIKE CONTEMPORARY ART

Oslo DAVIS
Australia 1972—

The Missing Bit from
    Sidney Nolan's Ned Kelly
    (1946). From Davis's series
    'Improvements on Australian Art'
2014 Melbourne
oil on canvas

'I'm over winter.'

Drawing the National Gallery of Victoria

Overheard at the Melbourne Festival

In 2008, *The Age* got me to hang around art lovers and festival-goers and eavesdrop on what they were saying.

(Needless to say, it put me off the cultural scene for years.)

Melbourne Writers Festival

The Game!

GET IN

Wait forever in the line to the toilets, which turn out to be the Anh Do book-signing queue.
MISS A TURN

GET OUT

Sleep with a festival volunteer, get free tickets to Mitchell Starc's book reading.
RETURN TO THE START

Develop a cold sore after sharing a spliff with a poet at an anthology launch in a freezing warehouse.
DON'T LEAVE THE HOUSE FOR THREE WEEKS

Jonathan Franzen compliments your hand-knitted orange-bellied parrot jumper.
ADVANCE TWO PLACES
(Or *MOVE BACK THREE* if you think he was being sarcastic.)

Helen Garner misspells your name when she signs your book.
MOVE BACK ONE PLACE

Sleep with a publisher, score a three-book deal.
ADVANCE TWO PLACES

Some jerk hogs question time.
TRASH THE JOINT

Draw attention to yourself by choking on wedge of kabana at an impromptu spoken-word jam, get invited on stage to perform.
MOVE BACK ONE PLACE

Collapse with joy when George Megalogenis briefly glances your way.
ADVANCE FIVE PLACES, FLOATING ON AIR

Festival keynote is by Malcolm Roberts.
QUIT POPULAR CULTURE, BECOME KELP FARMER

Bemoan the fact Australian fast bowler Mitchell Starc has published another stratospherically successful kids' picture book.
MOVE BACK ONE PLACE & GIVE UP ON WRITING ALTOGETHER

Get sucked into a two-hour session on OECD parallel importation rules.
MOVE BACK THREE PLACES

Miss out on asking Sally Rooney an audience question because some annoying boomer drops dead halfway through his lengthy opinion on something irrelevant.
MOVE BACK ONE PLACE

Down on Docklands

Have we all been too hard on Docklands? For a while now Melburnians have taken bucketloads of pleasure in bullying our newest suburb, like a four-year-old might his baby brother. It's a fun game, hating on Docklands, and, like good bullying, one that doesn't require any actual familiarity with the victim.

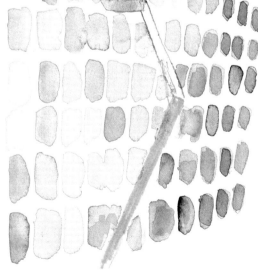

MOST PEOPLE I KNOW WOULDN'T be caught dead in Docklands. The place is a conglomeration of empty fusion restaurants, a dead Ferris wheel in the middle of nowhere and cheap all-day parking. If Docklands were a typeface it'd be Comic Sans. If it were a biscuit, the saccharine Orange Slice – not your first pick from the plate.

Even one of our lord mayors said: 'At the micro level it doesn't work', and that it lacks the 'social glue' of other suburbs. Swinburne housing researcher Professor Terry Burke, an obvious fan of action filmmaker Michael Bay, spoke for all of us when he said: 'They should blow it up and start again.'

But there's got to be something redeeming about the tarted-up, multi-billion-dollar former West Melbourne Swamp. Those quotes are from more than a decade ago – it's now home to more than 10,000 people, 72,000 people work there and the average age of residents is a funky thirty-one, five years younger than the Melbourne average. Maybe it's not so bad now?

To find out, I actually went to Docklands to talk to people who had consciously made an effort to go there, to do some sketching and to see if there was any basis for all the negativity.

My walk started at Southern Cross Station on a fine midweek winter day, and followed Collins Street over Batman Hill down into Docklands proper. Bruce Armstrong's eagle, Bunjil, perched in the middle of noisy, criss-crossing Melbourne traffic, looked over a horde of grim-faced, black-coated office workers. They were on their way to their Docklands office cubicles and looked like an updated version of John Brack's *Collins St., 5 p.m.*

I joined them as they walked past the swankily refurbished old Railway Goods Shed that now looks like MI5 from *No Time to Die*. Places Victoria, the agency that oversaw the development of Docklands, used to be in there. They reckoned by 2025 the whole place will be completed and will have cost $17.5 billion.

I then cut across to the water, passing public art by Emily Floyd and Mikala Dwyer, a basketball court and a community-services building unoriginally called The Hub. A bit further on, a cafe rudely blocks John Kelly's *Cow up a Tree*.

It's a stunningly beautiful blue morning on the dock; the yachts, the distant Bolte Bridge pylons and gigantic white cumulonimbus are perfectly reflected across a radiant harbour. Then the mood is shattered when I see a nearby seagull pecking at a sizeable puddle of what looks like human chunder.

At the cafe I accidentally meet artist Mark Stoner.
Mark and his friend Peter are in neck-to-toe cycling lycra
and have stopped for a flat white. Both are even-handed in
their assessment of Docklands, while acknowledging the place's
mistakes ('Docklands Stadium; too cut off from the CBD;
too much land given over to developers').

'There's no future in blame,' Mark says. 'It will evolve,
grow. It's only been around for a few years. Mistakes are an
inevitable part of getting it right.'

In 2011, Mark completed the *The River Runs Through It*
installation near ANZ's headquarters in Docklands. It's one
of the few responsive works of public art there that doesn't
look like it was just dropped in by aliens. Mark and Peter
make me ashamed of hating on Docklands so much, and
I resolve to seek out the good in the place.

Harbour Town, Docklands' shopping mall further west, brings me back to earth. Pauline, Anne and Jessie, pensioners just off a coach from South Australia, are looking for a place to sit and eat. 'Adelaide is busier than this on a Sunday!' says one of them, maybe Jessie. They all laugh and roll their eyes. 'So dead!'

Shoppers at Harbour Town look miserable, lost. Outside TunzaFun, a video-game centre just down from a glow-in-the-dark mini golf course, seven or eight Asian tourists fumble a big map. Further on, an empty men's clothing store sells clothes for men who, it seems, still think it's 1997. A bored shop assistant smiles at me, but her eyes are dead, like a lion in a cruddy zoo.

The struggle of the retailers here is well documented, but all things considered this mall is no worse than other malls across Melbourne. It's just more out of the way.

On the other side of Harbour Town is the Icehouse skating rink and the Wonderland Spiegeltent. On this weekday, only Costco seems to have any significant foot traffic. Wonderland Junior, a sorry-looking sideshow alley, is closed, and a nearby life-size T-rex (not listed on the public art map) is partially falling apart. Someone's put an empty bottle of Bundy in its mouth.

The Melbourne Star Ferris wheel was decommissioned in 2021 after more than a decade of operation. One of the largest observation wheels in the world, the Star was killed by Covid. Not that there was a lot to observe on this side of the city. Leah Cripps, a tourist from Bendigo, told *The Age*, 'My son was a little bit bored, only because it was going pretty slow.' In 2009 a couple were photographed engaged in a raunchy tryst in one of the cabins. But as someone who looks at it from the west, the wheel was an anchor that balanced Melbourne's skyline; it made sense for it to be there. And at night its jazzy lights made you feel Melbourne was *on*, like it was all happening.

Walking around, I meet Lyn, who's on the hunt for a long evening dress. Lyn's down from the country and shopping here because the 'city's too busy'. Lyn reckons this Harbour Town is not as good as the Harbour Town in Surfer's Paradise, and I wonder if she thinks the Harbour Towns are part of a chain. Maybe they are?

Near a bronze sculpture of an embarrassingly saucy-looking Kylie Minogue in NewQuay, I talk to Queenslanders Kyle and Chanese, a young couple who used to live in Docklands but have returned to see 'how the old neighbourhood is going'.

Kyle's memory of living there is of the wind, and he sends the mood of our pleasant chat into darker territories when he unexpectedly mentions that he was standing on his balcony the same day the wind blew that wall down on Swanston Street, killing three people.

Docklands was famous for underground rave parties in the 1990s. Thousands of clubbers in tracksuits danced in sheds that later would be razed for apartment blocks. Near one of the remaining sheds, I talk to an old Romanian man, also wearing a tracksuit, who's got a fishing line in the water. He shows me lots and lots of photos on his old Nokia of the brim and mullet he's caught there. I'm amazed at a picture of a 7-kilo snapper, and amazed even more at the massive storage capacity of his crappy old phone. 'I'm here three, four hours a day. Even caught salmon,' he says. 'You like to see picture of salmon?'

Victoria Harbour, a newer section of Docklands, where Collins and Bourke streets literally meet, is still being developed by Lend Lease, and there are a lot of cocky construction guys hanging around. For my money, Victoria Harbour is the prettier side of Docklands (I like the weird green grassy knoll especially), but the young guns working in real-estate marketing have taken over: billboards scream hyperbole and bad grammar alongside poorly photoshopped pictures of utopian living. It reads a bit like your cashed-up bogan brother-in-law trying to get you to come round and check out his awesome new deck.

Among the construction mess is a library, Docklands' highlight and my destination for the day. The little-known lending library, clunkily named The Dock, is a $23 million collaboration between Melbourne City Council, the state government and Lend Lease. It has ping-pong tables, a 3D printer, a cafe, free wi-fi, video games and a gallery. There are books there too.

Reclining in one of the modernist chairs on the top floor of the library, cocooned in the warm womb of a state-of-the-art designer building made of glass and wood, it's easy to imagine yourself as one of the filthy rich who can afford a luxurious Docklands penthouse with million-dollar harbour views. All I need now, I think to myself, eyes closed, afternoon sun licking my cheeks, is a cigar, some scotch and one of those foot-massage machines.

My head's a little groggy from all the walking and air and junky architecture, but it's clear enough for me to realise, ironically, that what I am liking most about daggy new Docklands is that it is so unpopular. It's an oasis just ten minutes by a free tram from the intensity of downtown Melbourne. It isn't exactly tons of fun at the moment, but it will get better, as Mark Stoner said. Better than Adelaide on a Sunday, at least.

Melbourne Miscellany

Illustrated moments you most likely missed
(described in haiku form)

At the Melbourne Zoo

Kimya totally
Blanks kid behind glass. Strolls off
Nowhere. Disgruntled.

At Highpoint Shopping Centre

Lifeless mannequins
Loiter nude out front Sportscraft.
Plastic and awkward.

Duo of shoppers
Smirk, raise eyebrows. Minimal
Genitalia.

At the Royal Botantic Gardens

Asian tourist snaps
His perfectly posed sweetheart.
Lays down flat and low.

Unbeknownst, garden staff
In tight green shorts mimic him
Waggishly. Grebe squawks.

In Elwood

Kind of splendid how
It crumpled blithely, like a
Shoebox. (No-one died.)

In North Melbourne

Poised yet timorous,
The whippet sets its brittle
Paw on Birkenstock.

In Carlton

Lazy reprobate
Crudely jammed catalogues in
Letter-slots' pursed lips.

In Glen Iris

This is how he parked.
Just ducked in for a banh mi.
White male, mid-twenties.

At Preston Market

Bin of iceberg leaves.
Lamentably close to the
Still viable ones.

At the Keilor Park
Remote Control Club

Fully grown man fangs
His RC buggy. Tara's
Home with the toddler.

At Avondale Heights

Radio says it's
Thirty-four degrees. Tai chi
Man wears a jumper.

Rent Me

Some FOR LEASE boards around Melbourne
you might have missed

Pure Apartment Porn

This Elon Musk–designed residence has a weekly rent equal
to that of a late model Hyundai Getz. It's what Madonna could
afford, had her last three albums sold. Plug in the NBN, turn on
the split system or accidentally touch the touch-free Zip taps and
we'll take your bond. The brass floors are ornamental, so keep
off! The spectacular balcony views are pay-per-view.

That's About the Size of It

Attention, agoraphobes, this one's for you! Our genius architects have somehow crunched a 2LDK into something akin to South Vietnam's Cu Chi tunnels. No need for furniture! Ideal for a slim, friendless contortionist. Kind of like 'The Hole' in Barwon Prison, but with rent. The kitchen is one of those bushwalking cookers rested on your knees. Bring your iPhone right up to your eyes, et voilà: widescreen TV!

Honey, Did You Hear Something?

This extremely affordable, spacious, clean and modern home is a noise sponge. And there's noise-a-plenty around! Upstairs, steel-capped-shoe-wearing neighbours rumba on particle board floors. Old insomniac over the way spot-welds corrugated iron with a rotary vane compressor. The triplets in number six have oboe lessons via Zoom every night with their teacher in Brussels. And the second your head hits the pillow, a mob of New Zealand backpackers three suburbs away on Inkerman Street crank up Fat Freddy's Drop. Feel the bass!

Breathe In the Nature!

Connect with the elements in this uninsulated, airy bungalow. Open plan like a carport. (Actually, it is a carport; you literally park your car beside the couch.) The water pressure relies on the tide. Throw away your essential oil diffusers; there's an aluminium smelter next door! Like wildlife? This place is practically Healesville Sanctuary! Except the koalas are brown rats and the native birds are chunky horseflies. Pigeon-fanciers will adore the family of common bronzewings that'll roost nightly on your bedhead. Such a sweet, cooing lullaby to send you off!

Well Read

Melbourne is a UNESCO City of Literature, whatever that means.

Walking Melbourne

Drawings done for a magazine article on
trekking around the inner city's trails

Meanwhile, on
St Kilda Beach

Where smoking is
compulsory, apparently

OSLO

Edinburgh Gardens

Sometimes the picnickers booze on a little too long. And the fire-twirling carnie crew with their bongo-playing pals are a little too scantily clad. Other days the dub is too loud. Or you get hit by a frisbee (or you roll your ankle on a broken umbrella, trying to catch a frisbee). Or someone's got their staffy off the lead and it's in everyone's stuff.

BUT EDINBURGH GARDENS IS BIG ENOUGH for you to find your own shady patch, to hide with a book. Or partake in a spliff. Or some smooching. Or, if you don't mind feeling too much like a wanker, set up an easel and do some *en plein air* painting. And there's a bowls club nearby if that's to your liking. And the Gardens are central enough to draw in your friends from the surrounding overpriced share-house suburbs.

I'm not sure there's anything else like it in Melbourne.

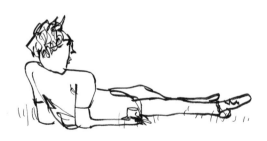

At the Dog Park

Reporting from the West Footscray dog park

Before I owned a dog, I used to think dog parks were nothing more than a fenced-off dog toilet. Now, with Pluto, my blue-and-tan Aussie terrier, I'm at my local dog park every day and have since given up my fear of catching ringworm. What's more, I now enjoy the weird camaraderie between us dog lovers.

MOST OWNERS KEEP TO THEMSELVES. They text, smoke, jog with prams. Some drink beer while their dogs do their thing. But when I ask them about their furry little companions, the spell is broken and they practically go into raptures. One man told me he got his cream-and-tan Jack Russell–Silky cross eight years ago from a shelter. 'Bobby's on time share. One month with me, one month with my ex.' How's he like that, I ask. 'It was tough at the start but he now knows he's going to get spoiled each month.'

Another guy told me his dog survived the Black Saturday bushfires. 'The property was lost but Audrey and her ten sibling pups were saved.' Audrey is a six-year-old Airedale terrier. 'Some of the other pups got names like Ash and Cinder, as you'd expect.'

Compared to the empty football oval adjacent, this dog park is often heaving. Sometimes there can be as many as forty dogs tearing about, sniffing each other, chasing frisbees, jumping up on people, nipping, rolling in something. The owners of Zelda, a sprightly mini foxie, reckon the council should do something about the park, which is a bit of a mangy dust bowl. 'It's like they don't care about parks that are not for humans.'

Many humans I talked to that evening had come straight from work, still in their high-vis vests or good shoes. A middle-aged woman I met explained how she got her whippet, Floyd, through a program called Mates for Inmates at the prison where she works. Run by Melbourne City Mission, the program aims to rehabilitate both dogs and criminals at the same time. Floyd was sleek and placid when I patted him, and I wondered if the woman was an ex-con and what she might have done time for.

Later on, I met Lucy, a two-year-old purebred black lab who used to work for Australia Customs. 'She was training to be a sniffer dog but failed,' her owner told me. 'Apparently she's got a "fluffy elbow", a type of arthritis. But I can't see anything wrong with her. She's just as rude as other dogs.'

The last dog I met was Charlie, a three-year-old
King Charles–Maltese cross whose claim to fame is that he
once licked Kevin Rudd's hand. 'It was during his last election
campaign. Look, I have a photo,' Charlie's owner said. But he
took ages finding it on his phone and it was getting late so I
told him I had to go. 'Sorry, mate, the dog wants to get home.'

The Big Dance

Richmond broke a 37-year drought when they beat Adelaide to
win the 2017 AFL Premiership. Everyone in Melbourne was a
Tigers supporter that day, including most of the 100,021-strong
crowd at the MCG, who did their best to ignore Richmond's
absurd away guernsey: yellow with a black slash.

Girls Onside

Melbourne, city of soccer

FOOTBALL, OR SOCCER AS WE USUALLY CALL IT IN OUR HOUSE, IS THE MOST POPULAR SPORT PLAYED BY KIDS IN MELBOURNE

UGH!

48.7% SOCCER 30.5% BASKETBALL 25.7% CRICKET 20.5% NETBALL 17.9% AUSTRALIAN RULES FOOTBALL 30.3% DANCING

* PERCENTAGE OF KIDS AGE 6 TO 13 WHO PARTICIPATE IN THESE ACTIVITIES

MELBOURNE'S WEATHER
IS PERFECT FOR
WATCHING SPORTS

MY DAUGHTER SCANS THE PAPER EVERY DAY FOR WOMEN'S SOCCER NEWS

'Time finally comes for Matildas'

'Melbourne Victory enjoy life at the top'

'Sam kerr nominated for Fifa player of the year'

'Teen sensation named alongside Matildas stars in World Cup squad'

'Matildas now ranked 6th in the world'

'Matildas paid a pittance compared to Socceroos'

OBSESSIVE BALL JUGGLING IS

TURNING MY DAUGHTER

INTO A BALL-JUGGLING ZOMBIE

(AT LEAST SHE'S NOT ON FORTNITE)

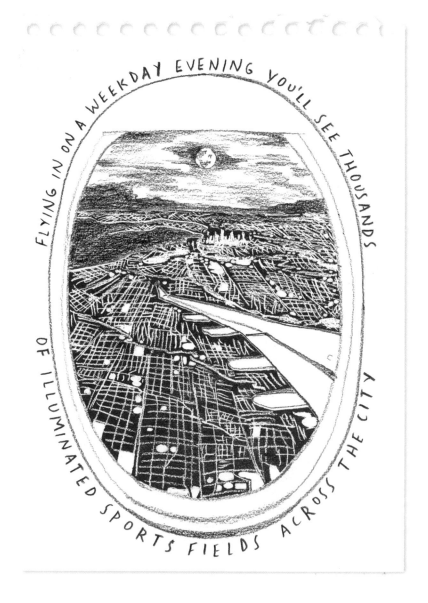

FLYING IN ON A WEEKDAY EVENING YOU'LL SEE THOUSANDS OF ILLUMINATED SPORTS FIELDS ACROSS THE CITY

THE DRIVE TO TRAINING TAKES US PAST

SOME OF MULTICULTURAL MELBOURNE'S

MOST EXOTIC RESTAURANTS

AT TRAINING, SOME OF THE DADS LIKE TO HELP OUT IN GOAL

I NEVER IMAGINED MY DAUGHTER WOULD COME TO SHARE A COMMON INTEREST WITH A COMMUNITY OF ETHNICALLY DIVERSE MELBOURNE MEN

BUT HER CLUB IS MADE UP OF
GIRLS WHOSE FAMILIES HAVE COME
TO MELBOURNE FROM ALL OVER

(LIKE SINGAPORE, ERITREA,
ALBANIA, JAPAN, FOR EG.)

'ETHNIC DIVERSITY' IS, HOWEVER, THE LAST THING THE GIRLS CARE ABOUT WHEN THEY'RE 2-0 DOWN

AFTER THE GAME (WE WON 4-3 AGAINST SOUTH) THERE'S THE OBLIGATORY GREASY SNAG AT THE CLUB BARBIE

FOLLOWED BY A PISTACHIO AND RICOTTA CANNOLI ON THE WAY HOME

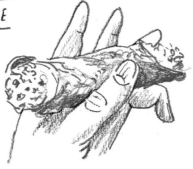

OSLO DAVIS

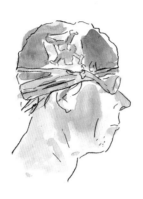

All at Sea

I understand that little surge of cockiness you might get when you say: 'I swim.' What do you do for exercise? I swim. Really? Yeah, just a few times a week. It's no big deal. Saying you swim is a humblebrag, like saying you drive a Volvo. Running is common, but swimming is fancy: you strip down to the bare minimum and dunk yourself in a contained expanse of water. It involves commitment, effort, uncomfortableness and rewards.

I SWIM AT THE VICTORIA UNIVERSITY POOL in Footscray. It's a 25-metre, eight-lane, deep indoor pool that hangs out from a hill and looks out over sports fields, the Maribyrnong River, the Flemington Racecourse and the Melbourne Showgrounds. From the end of lane seven – my favourite lane – you can see uni students doing nothing much under the pine trees in Footscray Park. At certain times of the day, sunlight beams in through the portholes under the water, making it feel magical, like you're in a resort pool.

I go there at about three in the afternoon, when it's at its quietest. ABC *Breakfast*'s Michael Rowland swims there too. Mostly freestyle. Slaps his skinny arms flat onto the surface of the water like they're a couple of sticks. I'm a poor swimmer. I stop a lot, maybe every two or three laps. My breathing is terrible and I have no rhythm. It's painful but in a good way, like eating spicy biryani.

Recently, in a moment of cockiness, I entered, for the first time, an ocean swimming competition. My editor at a newspaper liked the idea of my writing and drawing about the experience but he seemed concerned – was I up to it, fitness-wise? I allayed his fears by giving him my 'I swim' line, and said my skills from VU would transfer nicely to the ocean.

Ocean swimming is not unlike other minor sports in that organisers claim it's one of Australia's fastest growing sports. In Victoria there are more than forty organised open-water swims in a calendar year. Most are held in the ocean, with a handful in rivers and lakes. Lorne's famous Pier to Pub is recognised by the *Guinness World Records* as the world's largest ocean water swim, with 5000 swimmers competing.

The annual Danger 1000 Ocean Swim, which I entered, consists of 2.5 km, 500 m and 1000 m events, the last of which is broken into twelve age divisions. Typically, more than 2000 people pay about $53 each to compete, which I thought was a bit steep, but I guess you get a free T-shirt, swimming cap and drawstring bag.

(The 'Danger' Series gets its name from Torquay's Point Danger, not from the dangers of ocean swimming generally, although a white pointer was spotted at the beach in a recent November, which added a somewhat macabre suitability to the event's slogan: 'Dare yourself!')

Walking down to my race I bumped into Ben Birchall, an old friend I hadn't seen for ages, who told me he'd just completed the massive 2.5 km swim. I had no idea he did these swims. 'Took me just under fifty minutes,' he said coolly. I would have been less surprised if he told me he could speak fluent Portuguese.

'What I love about ocean swimming,' he said, 'is that there is no gravity in the water, so even if you're carrying extra weight you can still swim.' (I tried to not take this personally.) 'The repetition of movement, counting of strokes and lack of external stimulus makes it a really meditative experience.'

Standing on the shoreline before my first ocean swim, I was feeling anything but zen. I was anxious about not being able to rest every couple of laps, and there'd be no wall every twenty-five metres to push out from. My shoulder was sore from a frisbee strain, I had sunscreen in my left eye and the puff I took of my Ventolin had yet to kick in. Also, this was the first time I'd worn my hot pants–style Speedos outside VU, so the top halves of my thighs were bone white and this made me look like a creep.

I met an older guy named Mike who said this was also his first ocean swim. Mike's white whiskers and small, tidy stature made him look like a wizened Jack Russell terrier. I made a secret plan to stick close to Mike, just in case things went pear-shaped, for either of us.

Before sounding his hooter, marshal Michael Leigh told everyone if they found themselves in trouble they should put their hand up and someone would fish them out. 'It'll be a waste of your entry fee,' he said, 'but still a worthwhile donation to the surf club.'

Then everyone sprinted in. If you pine for that moment in a nightclub when the fire alarm goes off and everyone stampedes towards the exit, then competitive ocean swimming is for you. At least that's what the manic start of the race of the Danger 1000 Ocean Swim was like. Had I entered the 500 metre event not to overcome my fear of death by drowning but to die instead by being kicked in the face?

I let the kids in fluoro and old people with loose skin dolphin-dive ahead of me. Ben was right when he said the starts are 'like jumping in a washing machine full of bowling pins'. This was a far cry from my serene afternoon swims where I had the lane to myself.

The bay looked flat, but down at water level the 44-knot winds blew up plenty of spray and this made it tricky to find a rhythm, so I freestyled with my head out of the water. I was soon breathing in short breaths that were continually interrupted by mouthfuls of spray. My goggles fogged up and this brought on claustrophobia. The water was sandy brown and unnerving, and this induced a low-level panic, which I had to push down lest it consume me. If I'd had a tail it would have been tucked in, protecting my shrunken testicles. (At this point I was also cognisant that I was quite possibly losing my mind.)

A hundred metres out into Bass Strait I looked around for the nearest Surf Life Saving volunteer. The closest was a kid on a surf ski about 50 metres away, fiddling with his watch.

Mike was nowhere to be seen.

Obesity has tripled in Australia since 1990, and there was plenty of evidence of this in the crowds mooching about under Torquay's Norfolk pines. But the sleek, muscular swimmers on the beach looked like a new species of super humans, or insects. Even the overweight swimmers looked fit. A few of the older swimmers I met voluntarily told me about the benefits of ocean swimming, including how it boosts your immune system, eases aches and pains and even revs up your sex drive. (You don't need to hear this last factoid from an octogenarian who's just swam 1000 metres, although it's cute that they don't mind telling you.)

On this day, Marijke Alderson won the Warriors 70+ division, swimming 1000 metres in nineteen minutes. Her effervescent skin had a glow that women thirty years her junior fly to beauty salons in Koh Samui to get. She told me she liked swimming in ocean comps because it was 'a controlled environment' (read: shark patrols). Bruce Allender, who came second in the 70+ men's race, started telling me about swimming in big surf, but we were walking barefoot across a stretch of scorchingly hot sand and I couldn't concentrate and I actually started to cry a little bit.

David Bell, another guy I met, finished his 1000 metre swim in just over twenty minutes. 'It was my first Danger Ocean swim since having a heart attack last year!' Being around these fit old dudes, I found myself automatically sucking my guts in, like I was on a date.

In the water I struggled past another teenager on a ski, who looked down at me, bemused. Through her youthful eyes I saw how un-co I looked. She said, 'You're doing great,' which under any other circumstance I would have taken as patronising.

Rounding the first of two 6-foot pink buoys, I immediately felt the wind behind me and resumed freestyling. And there was little Mike, about 50 metres ahead but way offcourse, like he was heading straight for the carpark. Get back, Mike! Don't waste your energy, man!

After the last buoy I pointed my head towards the big blue inflatable finish-line arch, 200 metres away on the beach. With freestyle coming easier now, and the panic gone, I was in survival mode, focused on bringing it home. This was surely going to be one of the greatest survival stories of our time. Maybe they'd do an *Australian Story* on me?

Swimmers started standing up and when I put my foot down I realised I was in waist-deep water. I lugged my sorry carcass up the sand to the finish line. When Mike came in ten seconds later we congratulated each other, like we'd just survived a ferry sinking.

Back in Footscray, I hook my toes over the edge of platform
seven, put one hand out and on top of the other and sucked in
as much air as I can. In my mind I hang in the air for minutes
before punching into the water. Under here I can see stuff.
I scoop down before levelling out, my target is the porthole
down the end. A few lanes over, scuba divers bob across the
bottom like dugongs, and farther still the famous ABC journo
continues to whack the water.

Melbourne Sketchbook

Drawings from the trenches

VIEW OF THE SOCCER AT AAMI PARK

ALL FEAR THE DRIVER WITH HIS* ARM FLOPPED OUT THE WINDOW

* AND IT IS ALWAYS A MAN

THE FAMOUS BISON AT WERRIBEE ZOO!

WHAT BIRD IS THAT?
BRUNETTIUS SCAVENGER VENARI

(THE COMMON BRUNETTI SCAVENGER)

STUFFED TISSUE UNDER CAFE TABLE LEG, OPTIMIST

PITY THE CUTE LITTLE FLUFFY DOG

STUCK WITH ITS DRUG-FUELLED OWNERS

COURTNEY BARNETT

SOME JERK
FILMING HER
FOR AT LEAST
FOUR SONGS

AT THE NGV:

EDGAR DEGAS' 'DANCER LOOKING AT THE
BLOCK OF LEGO EMBEDDED IN HER FOOT'

ELEGANT
PLANTS
AT AN
INELEGANT
SHOPPING MALL.
(HIGHPOINT)

(TOOK ME JUST THREE RIDES

ON THE ESCALATOR TO DRAW THIS)

BALLAD OF THE FALLEN NON-DECIDUOUS LEAF

WHAT THE HELL
AM I DOING
DOWN HERE?

_0_

MAN AT KENSINGTON
CAFE LEANS TO
THE RIGHT

_0_

TO KEEP OUT OF THE SUN.

Greetings from the

Flinders St Station
Food Court

BREAKING NEWS

FIRST LEAF OF SPRING EMERGES!
(CORNER OF VICTORIA & PEEL STREETS)

CROUCHING ATTENBOROUGH,

SLEEPING TERRIER.

A WANKER* OF REAL ESTATE STAFF
HAVING A MEETING IN A SMALL CAFE.

* THE COLLECTIVE NOUN

(TODAY'S QUIZ)

FOOT NOT _ON_ THE TRAIN SEAT BUT ON _THE SIDE_ OF _THE SEAT_.

THAT'S ME: SUBVERTING THE DOMINANT PARADIGM ONCE _AGAIN!_

STILL DRIVEABLE

(NOT MY CAR)

IF THERE IS ANY JUSTICE
IN THE WORLD, A WRECKING BALL

WILL FALL ON THE MERCEDES
ILLEGALLY PARKED IN THE

DISABLED SPOT AT MY DAUGHTER'S SCHOOL

NOT LOITERING, DRAWING

(POTTED FOLIAGE, HIGHPOINT)

END OF THE GAME

(CRUSHED PING PONG BALL)

NOBODY KNOWS I'M WALKING UP
THIS PARLIAMENT ST.N ESCALATOR

TO THE EXACT BEAT OF AN
AWESOME LCD SOUNDSYSTEM SONG

RAIN:1

INADEQUATE TRAIN STATION DESIGN: 0

Through the Peepholes

Last week as I was walking through the city it occurred to me that I hadn't seen a construction site peephole in a while. This wasn't such a big deal – I don't particularly have an interest in watching construction workers per se – until I realised I also hadn't seen in ages one of those daggy guys who stop to look through the peepholes.

CONSTRUCTION SITE PEEPHOLES, those funny little windows in the hoardings around massive building sites, used to be everywhere in Melbourne. Men – it was mostly men, in my experience – would comically stand and look through these portholes at stuff, hogging the whole frame. What they saw was a magnificent image of construction, projected through the peephole onto the back of their retinas, like a camera obscura, that then in turn tickled the neurons in their brain.

Today's peephole-less hoardings give off a sinister vibe, like the high walls of an embassy. And not knowing what's going on behind these walls gets my back up; I go a bit bolshie. *It's our city, our streets, our spaces – we have a right to look! What have you got to hide? What's going on in there?!*

Site managers, I reckon, regard peepholes at best as an act of conciliation, and at worst as an altruistic gift they are under no obligation to provide. 'For safety reasons we can't open the site up, but we'll graciously let you look at it through this little hole. You can thank us later.'

But for the men on the street who lean in for a look, as well as for us casual observers, peepholes are the least a construction site can do to atone for the noise, messy footpaths and general ugliness they inflict on us.

During my city walking and drawing over the last few years, I've sketched that anonymous peephole perv a few times and have wondered about his backstory. Who is that fifty-something bloke glued to the footpath, kind of in the way, oblivious to the world rushing around him?

Is he a former construction worker? Perhaps he got fired, suffered a workplace injury or just had a gutful and up and quit? After a period of grieving, a breakdown, a divorce, a court battle and/or crippling back pain, has he returned to the peephole to get updates on what's going on? Or, more grandly, does he like to think he's bearing witness to the birth of a landmark? Seeing Melbourne's transformation in action? History wiped clean for a new future to take its place?

Or is he just an everyday Joe mooching around, skiving off work, marvelling at the men-ants in fluoro, the state-of-the-art machinery, the speed and slowness of progress, the mud, the mess, the problems, the problem-solving, the teamwork, the lifting, the hoisting, the drilling, the noise, the trucks?

They are building something amazing down there. They have removed a massive tooth from the gums of the city grid and are now digging deeper, ten levels down. Soon they will start to build. How will they do it? How did they get all that machinery down there? How will they get it all out? How will this building change the street, the city? What's going on?!

(And what of the construction workers themselves? Do they like the parade of perfectly framed heads up there at street-level admiring their work, and do they ever take time to stand and look back through the hole at us?)

Sadly, the peepholes and the men who looked through them are going, if not gone – it's the end of an era. Eventually, the tower will be built and the hoardings will move to another site where they may or may not let us stand, lean in and see what's going on.

Melbourne by Night

Drawings done on a summer-night sojourn into the CBD
with a writer for a newspaper article. Wouldn't necessarily
recommend it to anyone over twenty-three. Could've cut
the testosterone in the air with a knife. Lots of tight dresses
and full-throated screaming out of car windows. Everyone
tarted-up and trashy. Crouching and crying in gutters
about boyfriends called Deng. Don't make eye contact.
Certainly wasn't like that in my day.

Ugliness

Drawings I did for *After the Australian Ugliness* (NGV, 2021), which celebrated sixty years of Robin Boyd's iconic 1960 book. These drawings were inspired in style and tone by the architect and writer's own skilful and witty illustrations.

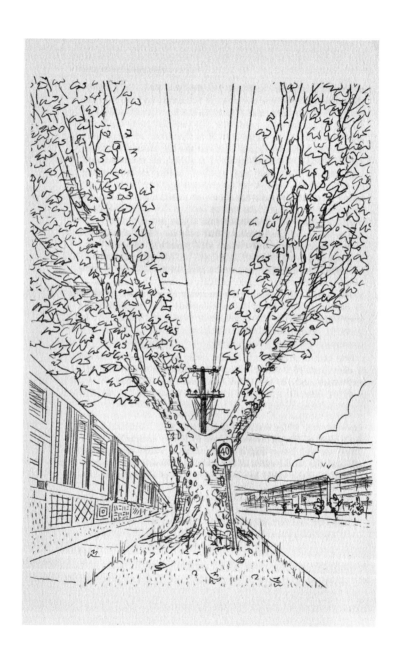

The Sole Milk-Bar Proprietor

Down the road from our house is the local milk bar. A well-stocked little shop conveniently smack-bang in the middle of our suburb.

Problem is, my wife and I are freaked out by the chubby little fifty-something bloke who runs the place. We can't put our finger on it, but he never says hello, thanks or anything, and his whole demeanour gives off such bad vibes it feels like he's on the verge of leaping the counter and running us through with a Stanley knife.

And, as the sole milk-bar proprietor in the area, this fifty-something has our suburb by the balls. Unless you get in the car and drive there's no way you're going to go anywhere else to buy your milk, your caster sugar or your after-dinner almond Magnum.

Lately my wife and I have been talking a lot about that bloke. About how he once dropped a twenty-cent coin down among the Extra chewing gum, and left it there. How he charged us $11.60 for some thickened cream. And how he spent ages trying to open a plastic bag with his thumbs, but then just chucked it to my wife, unopened.

We've previously spent a bit of time in Japan, so we've been imagining him trying to run a milk bar – a *konbini* – in Tokyo, where service standards are set ludicrously high and competition is cutthroat. He'd go belly-up in a flash.

But we also wonder if he, in moments of calm and reflection, feels remorse or shame, even, for his atrocious customer service? Maybe he has tried to change, but lacks the tools to do so? Or perhaps he's fully aware of the power he wields as our suburb's sole milk-bar proprietor?

Camberwell Market

THE WAY MY FAMILY AND I DO the Camberwell Market is we drive over at about nine, not too late, not too batshit early, and park under Woolies. Then the four of us split up, arranging to meet near the Rotary Club volunteers at the entrance in an hour. That's enough time, really. We usually bump into each other anyway – making the same joke at the same time that we don't know each other, pretend-ignoring each other. Then we either go our own way again, or lead each other to stuff we've found and discuss if we should get it or if it's too much, etc. Then we might split up again if there's still time left in the hour, before rendezvousing with our booty, or lack thereof. Then we drive home, stopping on the way at Suzuran, the excellent Japanese grocery and sushi shop, for snacks, cooking stuff, sashimi and maybe a little bottle of sake if I'm feeling flush.

A list of things I've *nearly* bought at the Camberwell Market:
    – an automatic Seiko 5 watch with a scratch on it
    – a wedding photo of the betrothed kissing in an apple
       grove, mounted in a luxuriously ornate frame
    – an antique wooden ladder
    – a Patagonia T-shirt with a stain on it that you could
       probably get out
    – a podium.

Overheard at Camberwell Market
Sunday, 9:30 a.m.

'I'm standing here. I'm standing here. At the entrance.
I'm looking at you. You're looking at me. I said you're
looking at me. I'm standing here.'

Overheard at Camberwell Market
Sunday, one p.m.

'Why don't you go away, have a think and then
ask yourself: how much am I willing to pay for
a fried-egg necklace?'

Pressing Matters

The Westall UFO

The truth is out there, on the Pakenham Line

When I was a Christian, my Sunday school teacher told me if I heard someone say my name but I didn't see who said it, then it was probably Jesus calling me. That happened to me a fair bit when I was six, apparently, but I didn't have that unnerving sensation for almost forty years ... until I went to Westall.

Did they come to simply harvest
pine cones for their air fresheners?

I came to
Westall in
peace

WESTALL IS A NONDESCRIPT SUBURB loitering in a void between Springvale and Clayton South. I drove down there on a 34-degree Tuesday morning last summer and parked on Rosebank Ave, the main drag with your typical B-grade suburban restaurants, milk bars and an oversupply of massage parlours. Greater Westall is all houses and industrial parks. Except for a pretty patch of native bush called Grange Reserve, there's no reason you'd put Westall on your bucket list.

But then again, as everyone knows, Westall's ominous claim to fame is that it's the location of Australia's biggest mass sighting of UFOs. Just before Easter in 1966, it's said that a UFO-shaped something flew low over the high school and landed in the Grange, leaving a perfect circle of cut, scorched grass before taking off again, pursued by three smaller unidentified craft. More than 200 school kids saw this extraterrestrial dance before later being told they didn't see anything.

Because of this you'd assume Westall would be cashing in big-time on its Roswell-esque notoriety. However, a quick look around revealed a place oblivious to the UFO-tourism goldmine it was sitting on. Where were the hokey UFO museums or shops selling alien merch? Or the posters for an annual interstellar street parade featuring the former child witnesses from '66 on the backs of utes, waving? There weren't even any shops emblazoned with tacky space motifs or UFO-related names. Where were the Alien Burgers? UFOrthodontists? Or Flying Sauces and Spices shops?

Westall was still strange, though, in a Twin Peaksy kind of way. And I felt a strangeness being there. In the heat of that Tuesday, the few people I saw moved about like extras on a set, rarely looking up as they performed menial actions: purposefully placing half-eaten chicken burgers in the bin, pressing buttons on the ATM, bringing their arms up to look at their watches. Two youths mooched around in identical T-shirts printed with 'Graves RIP 2011–2017'. I thought I heard one of them, or someone, say my name.

I went into Westall's only lawnmower shop and asked a middle-aged white guy in tight shorts if he knew anything about the aliens. 'Nah nothing, sorry, mate. Nothing like them round here.' I realised he might have thought I was talking about refugees so I tactfully reminded him about 1966, but he drew a blank.

Same with the Asian-Australian proprietor of Westall Charcoal Chicken. When I asked him if the UFO brings in the tourists, he put down a crumbled cutlet and looked into the middle distance, eventually saying, 'Oh, the UFO from the 1990s?' I corrected him on the date. 'Really?' he said. 'I'm pretty sure it was, like, 1995.' He then claimed to have no idea what I was talking about.

As I left, his wife looked at me and said something to her husband in a low tone, but her words were lost in the sizzle of the fryer.

Outside, a jittery pensioner struggled to lift himself out
of his Toyota Echo, banging his door repeatedly against the
polished side of an exquisitely seamless Mercedes Benz. It was
a miracle he didn't set off the alarm. I purposefully placed
my half-eaten chicken burger in the bin and got up to ask
Grandpa some questions – namely, was he one of the teenagers
who raced across the field in fevered pursuit of the UFO? –
but when I looked up he'd vanished. He may have popped into
the Rosebank Oasis massage parlour for a lomilomi, but that
seemed unlikely …

Down at Grange Reserve, ground zero, I made my way under slender pines that groaned in the heat. If Westall was to fess up about the UFO, surely it would be here.

Infographics on the toilet walls described the Earth's solar system and the lunar landing, suspiciously ignoring the UFO. However, someone had built a blue-topped, hard-edged UFO in the playground. It was a cute gesture, but a lazy simulacrum of the real thing; multiple witnesses have said the silver spacecraft looked as if it 'had come out of a mould' and had 'no seams, no joins'.

Alone and willingly, I climbed up into the UFO through its centre hole. It was not the hot box I expected, but there was a perceptible atmospheric shift, like when you go into a soundproof booth and shut the door. When I sat down and my pulse settled I heard the distant drone of lawnmowers, which I hadn't heard out on the tanbark. A thin oblong shard of light pivoted into my eyes through an empty Corona bottle.

When I came to my senses it was almost two. Council gardeners pretended I wasn't there as I walked over to a little info panel that explained (finally!) the UFO event. It offered explanations that involved silver balloons and high-level nuclear testing, but the font was quite small and I had left my reading glasses in the car so I couldn't really read it.

Back up at the shops, a skinny man carrying a lighter asked me for the time, so I lifted my arm up to look at my watch. The youths in 'Graves RIP' T-shirts were still there muttering names. Driving away, I saw a crow in my rear-view mirror picking up a piece of chicken burger from the bins.

The Three Rs

Drawings for Triple R 102.7 FM, a Melbourne independent radio station

In Reservoir (2015)

My artist friends get residencies in New York, Kyoto, Reykjavik. I got one in Reservoir. Further out than Courtney Barnett's 'Depreston', Reza is Melbourne's loveable mongrel suburb that used to have a monstrous rail-and-road intersection you could see from the moon.

A WHILE BACK, I RODE the South Morang train up there every day for a fortnight to draw the natives, the fruits of which I turned into a little newspaper called *Reservoiria*.

When I was there, Reservoir was post-war and pre-gentrification. I suspect it's gentrified proper now. I saw a lot of property-developer wankers in suits, barking bad grammar into hands-free phones. But I mostly saw a Reservoir still full of old people comfortably dressed in slacks and beige cable-knit cardigans.

Mooching on street furniture, I felt like an aged-care nurse on an extended lunch break. Around me the infirm pushed trolleys and waited for buses, for the lights to change and for results to come back from radiology. The absence of mums with prams or kids on Edwardes Street led me to assume Reservoir was in the grip of a mysterious fertility disease, like in that movie *Children of Men* starring Clive Owen.

Near the library I met a retiree named Tai from the Cook Islands, who came to Reservoir thirty years ago. 'I've never been back, no need,' he told me, seemingly happy with himself.

Down the hill is Sargent's Cakes, a Reservorian institution, which, according to their sign, was voted the '#1 Cake Shop 1999, 2000 and 2001'. Past the Pole Princess, a glamorous pole-dancing school, is Phil's flower shop with an aviary in the window. 'Twelve months ago,' Phil said, 'my aviary at home blew over, so I brought my birds to work and spoonfed them back to health.'

At Edwardes Lake, kids swarmed over a big, old, decommissioned black train, like little ants on a bigger, older, decommissioned black ant. Among them towered David, a fifty-something who had come up from Northcote to specifically check out the A2 967 locomotive. 'I've been meaning to get up here for ages,' he said. To me it looked like a boring old steam train, but he was in raptures.

Nearby, I overheard power-walking women describing in detail disgusting operations they'd had.

In a street behind the park lives my old mate Louise Swinn, who moved out there years ago. 'It means we can have a bigger block … but it would be nice to be closer to the action.' Her garage is a writing studio suitable for writing a masterpiece, or completely losing your mind; there's not a lot in Reservoir to help you procrastinate.

But I like Reservoir, in the same way you like your nan, even though she's old and has no idea what a staycation is, despite having been on one for the last forty-three years. I also like the tyre swans on the front lawns that are extinct everywhere else, the easygoing vibe and the high-class hard rubbish.

On my last day there, I headed over to scungy-looking Broadway – the other main street, with newer immigrants, a rusty bingo hall and a famed Wall of Cheese. At the trendy Lady Bower cafe, I got a half-decent coffee. It was so packed with young people I felt like I was somewhere else, like I wasn't on an art residency in Reservoir.

Good Wine

Plonk you won't find at Dan Murphy's

Wateries

White. $7.30, 2020
Made from grapes grown in a
Cremorne easement that got
inadvertently tangled around a
police diver's wetsuit. Partially
drained of illicit substances, bottled
and submitted as evidence.

Cranbourne Plains

Whitish-Red. $5, 2019
A kooky wine, 'accidentally'
developed at the Cranbourne
Secondary College by a couple
of STEAM kids currently doing
time at the Malmsbury Youth
Justice Centre. Contains nutmeg.

Hospice Stay

Golden. $5, 2019
From grapes grown on a
decorative lattice in the courtyard
of the Puse Blouse Nursing Home.
Harvested by the arthritic fingers
of elderly Filipino war brides.
Real sour.

Tom's Good Route

Cream. $7, 2021
First and only batch from Tom
Harvey, celebrated MMA fighter.
Comes in two-litre PET bottles.
Hints of flat Pepsi, Deep Heat
and peptides.

Mudlover's Revenge

Murky. $6, 2001
This carp-infused brown booze
hails from Corner Inlet's mudflats
and is chock-a-block full of
seagrass pulp. (Comes with a free
strainer.)

Barbara's Fun

Fizzy. $9, 2020
Dubbed the 'sherbet', this wine
is made by injecting 150 psi of
baking soda into sugary grape
cordial. It'll make your eyes water.

Ian's Place

Red. $5, 2018
This exceptionally versatile
inebriant can be chugged
with any foodstuffs: from
pizza to chips to KFC. With
NutraSweet™.

Old Bastard

Deep Red. $4, 2015
This dense meal is made on
a boat near Warrnambool by
divorced, middle-aged squid
fishermen. Nice heated up.

Incarceration Red

White. $6, 2015
This firewater has that smell you
only get at Bunnings, and has
the consistency of two-stroke oil.
(Do not leave on the roof of your
car.) Illegal to buy, sell or drink.

Devonport Run

Red. $8, 2022
Bottled approximately
70 metres from where the
Spirit of Tasmania fuels up, this
ungainly Tasmanian red sports
hints of Mr Sheen and rust.

Libraryland!

Hanging out and drawing at the
State Library of Victoria

I HAVEN'T LOOKED AT THE STATS, but I reckon a major reason people spend hours in the State Library of Victoria, a big old place over the road from Melbourne Central, is because it has free wi-fi. I reckon this because I did a three-month Creative Fellowship there and spent a fair chunk of time looking at what everyone did, and then drawing them.

The SLV is not usually a place that one would engage with directly, unless you're a tourist or part of the maintenance crew. But when I was there I filled five big Moleskine sketchbooks with drawings of stuff I saw: galleries, paintings, people looking at paintings, sculptures, busts, the chairs in the domed La Trobe Reading Room, the library staff and the thousands of library users who tramped about, read, texted, chewed gum, slept and yabbered away into their phones.

I didn't have plans to do anything with my doodlings; I felt no compulsion to publish them and there wasn't a deadline or an editor breathing down my neck. Similarly, I didn't beat myself up if my drawings were wonky, weird or wrong. My goal was simply to enjoy the act of drawing.

So, I drew. I'd start off drawing something normal, like a power point or a clock, just to limber up. Then I'd play games, like, can I draw every person that walks past me in the next fifteen minutes? Can I draw that chair without looking at the page? I'd start drawing something normal but would then give it a silly twist at the end. That lady's hair looks like claws! Those guys are fish! Look – a knuckle dragger!

It wasn't all fun and games – the lure of the free wi-fi, Saul Steinberg books and a 24-hour news cycle made it tempting not to draw. But the pay-off from days of drawing was huge: I now have life, nonsense and the library itself captured in the pages of five Moleskines.

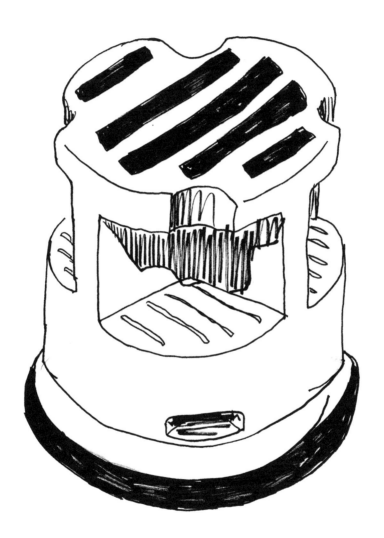

A Visual Expedition

A short while back, I was invited to explore and make
drawings in response to the State Library's flora and fauna
collection. Over a few weeks in the library and in its massive
online catalogue, I looked through thousands of books,
dried plant specimens, photos, assorted objects, maps,
visual diaries and art. You should do it too – there's some
pretty weird and wonderful stuff there.

THE CRITICALLY
ENDANGERED
HELMETED HONEY EATER,
IS VICTORIA'S BIRD EMBLEM

I LIKE TO THINK I LOOK LIKE
A HIGH COURT JUDGE!

JOHN GOULD'S
HELMETED HONEY EATER
HAS MORE OF A BOOFY MULLET

THE LIBRARY'S ARTWORK WALKS RIGHT OFF THE PAGE!

THIS RHINO IS FROM JOHN JOHNSTON'S 'HISTORIAE NATURALIS DE QUADRUPEDIBUS' AND IS MODELLED ON ALBRECHT DÜRER'S 1515 WOODCUT

Iris Germanique by Pierre-Joseph Redouté

(1759 — 1840)

A FRENCH FLOWER-PAINTER OF THE LATE 18TH EARLY 19TH CENTURY

(THE IRISES LOOK BETTER IN COLOUR... PIERRE-JOSEPH LESS SO)

JOHN GOULD, ORNITHOLOGIST, NAMED THIS
GOULDIAN FINCH
AFTER HIS WIFE ELIZABETH GOULD,
WHO DID A LOT OF THE
BIRD DRAWINGS FOR JOHN'S BOOKS.

YOU REALISE
'GOULDIAN'
ALSO REFERS
TO YOU, RIGHT?

WOMBAT.

ENGRAVER SAMUEL JOHN NEELE'S 1802 WOMBAT
(SERIOUSLY).

ETCHING OF THE MOMENT A SHARK WAS CAUGHT OFF BRIGHTON.
IT HAD BEEN TERRORISING SWIMMERS IN THE BATHS BY BASHING
INTO THE WALLS.

LATER IT WAS TAKEN TO M'COY'S LAB AND DRAWN
    FOR HIS 'PRODROMUS OF THE ZOOLOGY OF VICTORIA'.

CONSERVATOR
STILL LOOKING
AFTER JOHN JAMES
AUDUBON'S 'THE
BIRDS OF AMERICA'

Blackburnian Warbler

FROM A PHOTO OF A
TAXIDERMIST WORKING ON A DEAD
JAPANESE WAR PIGEON, 1945

AND HERE WORKING ON
A NOT-DEAD-YET FERRET *
* THIS MAY NOT HAVE ACTUALLY HAPPENED

JOHN GOULD'S DINGO

'WHETHER THE HEAD BE VIEWED AS A ZOOLOGICAL ILLUSTRATION OR AS A WORK OF ART, IT MUST BE EQUALLY ACCEPTABLE'
GOULD IN HIS 'MAMMALS OF AUSTRALIA'

Alfine reíla.
Right Chickweed.

ARTIST LUDWIG BECKER WAS PART OF THE BURKE & WILLS EXPEDITION. HE DID DRAWINGS OF EVERYTHING HE CAME ACROSS (CRABS, RATS, BUTTERFLIES ETC.). DREW MAPS AND KEPT A VISUAL DIARY.

HOWEVER, BURKE GOT CRANKY WITH HIM AND TOLD HIM TO QUIT DRAWING & STOP SLOWING EVERYONE DOWN. BECKER DIED ON THE TRIP FROM SCURVY IN 1861.

DON'T BE SILLY, DARLING—
THERE'S NO SUCH
THING AS A 'WEED'!

BRITISH NATURAL HISTORY PAINTER

FANNY ANNE CHARSLEY

LIVED IN MELBOURNE IN THE MID 1880s
AND DREW BEAUTIFUL WILD FLOWERS

Footscray Park

A few years ago, the Melbourne Victory soccer club wanted to turn the flat spaces of Footscray Park down by the Maribyrnong River into soccer fields. On the face of it, that seemed reasonable enough because most of that land was scungy and had poor drainage and no-one really went there, except for a few dog walkers and thousands of people every New Year's Eve for the fireworks.

BUT A LOT OF PEOPLE KICKED UP A STINK:
what gives a private company the right to take over and
lock up rare, open inner-city public space? The Maribyrnong
City Council polled the community on the matter and
found a third supported the soccer redevelopment, a third
were passionately against it and a third didn't care either way,
so they left the land as is.

But since then, Footscray Park has never appeared more
popular; the stoush was the perfect marketing campaign for
the park, and it has resulted in hundreds of people hanging
out there every day. It's as if nobody realised that this oasis,
this lovely botanical garden that runs down to wide-open
plains, was there. As Footscray continues to push apartment
towers into the sky, this heritage-listed park is now everyone's
newly rediscovered nature escape.

If you don't know the area, Footscray Park dramatically
pitches down from Ballarat Road, showcasing lush lawns
and flowerbeds, kookily shaped pines and an ornamental
duck pond, before arriving at a vast, soggy tundra, an uber-
cool kids' playground and the paved Maribyrnong River Trail.
(The Maribyrnong River itself is filthy. I was once there when
nine cars were pulled out from the riverbed.)

During Covid I spent a bit of time in Footscray Park, mostly walking my dog, tossing the frisbee with my wife and drawing trees on big sheets of slightly toothy paper from the comfort of a camping chair. I drew there to use up the dull days, but also to create simple drawings of nature that might inspire others, just as David Hockney's charcoal drawings of country lanes in Yorkshire have inspired me.

Forbury Park – 20-3-2020 OSW BAIT

FITZROY PARK. 3-5-2 OSLO DAVIS.

Footscray Park 26-3-2020 — OSW DAVIS

Goodbye to All That

ACCORDING TO SOME METRICS, Melbourne was, in recent years, the most locked-down city in the world. In an effort to turn our collective frown upside down, By All Means, an advertising agency, asked me to come up with a T-shirt design based on the title 'Greetings from Locktown'. Sales of this merch went on to raise more than $45,000 for Beyond Blue, a mental-health support organisation.

Today, I don't think I'm the only one who misses tiny aspects of those miserable lockdown days. The post-apocalyptic malaise that drowned our city kind of opened our senses to other stuff. It reminded me of the mind-emptyingly dull Sundays in the Tasmanian country town I grew up in, which in my older age I now kind of miss. Yet in locked-down Melbourne I was still able to order in the goat biryani from Dosa Hut or get a socially distanced delivery of books from the Sun Bookshop. Of course, nobody fully misses those 262 days in lockdown, but I could handle a one-off day of surreal city serenity every now and then.

Goodbye to
LOCKTOWN

Bio

Oslo Davis draws and writes for various publications and projects worldwide. This has included *The New York Times*, *The Guardian*, *The Monthly*, SBS and Readings. *Overheard*, Oslo's weekly eavesdropping cartoon, has been published in *The Age* since 2007. Oslo is also the author of the *This Annoying Life* colouring-book series, and he is a Walkley Award and American Illustration Award finalist. Oslo lives in Melbourne, obviously.

Thanks

Much of the work in this book would not have happened without the trust and support of the following editors and friends: Michelle Griffin, Lindy Percival, John Mangan, Nick Feik, Kylie Northover, Sophie Cunningham, Graham Meadowcroft, Tiarney Markus, Tash Reith-Banks, Annaliese Redlich, Megan Patty, Shannyn Higgins, Lucy De Kretser, Toby Cummings, Beth Wilkinson, Dan Rule and Emily Harms.

Special thanks to Sophy Williams, Akiko Chan and Lauren Carta at Black Inc. for their skills and smarts, and to Mika, Minami and Yuna Yamasaki for keeping me on my toes.

Notes

Many drawings and essays in this collection were previously published in a different form, including:

'Your Typical Melbourne Day': *Lindsay*, 2018.

'Art': *The Age*, 2012–2021; *The Monthly*, 2016; *Art Guide Australia*, 2019.

'Overheard at the Melbourne Festival': *The Age*, 2008.

'Melbourne Writers Festival: The Game!': *The Monthly*, 2019.

'Down on Docklands': *The Age,* 2015.

'Rent Me:' *Meanjin*, 2009.

'Walking Melbourne': *Royal Auto Magazine*, 2017.

'Meanwhile on St Kilda Beach': For the exhibition *Duality* curated by Shannyn Higgins, 2019.

'At the Dog Park': *The Age*, 2015.

'The Big Dance': *The Age*, 2017.

'Girls Onside': *The Guardian*, 2019.

'All at Sea': *The Age*, 2018.

'Swimming Through Traffic': Vinyl print of a watercolour illustration on a 23-metre C-Class Melbourne tram. Part of the Melbourne Festival's Art Tram project, 2018. Photo by James H. H. Morgan.

'Melbourne Sketchbook': *The Age* 2017–2020.

'Through the Peepholes': *The Age*, 2015.

'Melbourne by Night', *The Age*, 2015.

Ugliness: *After The Australian Ugliness*, National Gallery of Victoria and Thames & Hudson Australia, 2021.

'The Sole Milk-Bar Proprietor', *A Place Tells A Story*, 2010.

'Camberwell Market': *The Age*, 2016–2021.

'Pressing Matters': *The Age*, 2020.

'The Westall UFO': *The Age*, 2019.

'In Reservoir': *The Age*, 2016.

'Good Wine': *The Age*, 2008.

Published by Black Inc.,
an imprint of Schwartz Books Pty Ltd
22–24 Northumberland Street
Collingwood VIC 3066, Australia
enquiries@blackincbooks.com
www.blackincbooks.com

9781760643355 (paperback)
9781743822678 (ebook)

A catalogue record for this book is available from the National Library of Australia

Cover design by Oslo Davis
Text design and typesetting by Akiko Chan
Author illustration by Oslo Davis

Printed in China by 1010.